Witold Lutoslawski

Lullaby for Anne-Sophie

for violin and piano (1989)

Violin part edited by
Kaja Danczowska

Piano part edited by
Justyna Danczowska

Chester Music

LULLABY FOR ANNE-SOPHIE
na skrzypce i fortepian • for Violin and Piano

Ed.: Justyna Danczowska, Kaja Danczowska

WITOLD LUTOSŁAWSKI
(1913-1994)

* Znak chromatyczny odnosi się tylko do nuty, przy której jest umieszczony / An accidental refers only to the note it precedes

Poco meno mosso

Ancora meno mosso

poco f ___ *pp*

poco f ___ *pp*

rit.

With good reason, Witold Lutoslawski (1913–1994) regarded himself as a symphonist, although monumentality was a stranger to him. From time to time he composed miniatures for occasions such as birthdays, or as dedications to the memory of deceased friends. The manuscripts of a number of these hitherto unpublished miniatures are now part of the collection of the Paul Sacher Foundation in Basel. These include the *Lullaby for Anne-Sophie*, written in 1989. After *Chain II* for violin and orchestra (1985) and the orchestrated version of *Partita* (1988), this was the third piece composed for the violinist Anne-Sophie Mutter: the fourth, a violin concerto, was left unfinished at the composer's death.

Lullaby was a wedding gift for Mutter. Knowing that she suffered from insomnia, Lutoslawski handed her the manuscript with the comment, "In case you can't sleep, read this".

Although less than forty bars long, *Lullaby* is a composition full of beauty and at the same time refinement. In it we can hear all the qualities of late Lutoslawski: long-breathed melody, harmony based on meticulously constructed chords and irregular rhythm in the violin. Echoes of earlier works can also be heard, such as the steady, "cradling" triplet motion in the piano part at the beginning of the song, reminiscent of the first of the *Five Songs* to words by Illakowiczówna. Typical for Lutoslawski's style are the sequential repetition of short motives in the first half of the piece and also three- and four-note chords at the end which are a model example of a characteristic for this composer's pitch organisation. In its simplicity, *Lullaby* is a testament to great artistry which allowed Lutoslawski to build a work from a few ideas that is bewitching in its simplicity and subtlety. "This *Lullaby* has found a permanent place in my repertoire," said Anne-Sophie Mutter years later, "I always play it for an encore."

Krzysztof Meyer
translated by Lindsay Davidson

LULLABY FOR ANNE-SOPHIE
na skrzypce i fortepian • for Violin and Piano

Ed.: Kaja Danczowska

WITOLD LUTOSŁAWSKI
(1913-1994)

Poco meno mosso

Ancora meno mosso

* Znak chromatyczny odnosi się tylko do nuty, przy której jest umieszczony / An accidental refers only to the note it precedes

CH81807
ISBN 978-1-78305-332-2

Head office:
14–15, Berners Street,
London W1T 3LJ
England

Tel +44 (0)20 7612 7400
Fax +44 (0)20 7612 7549

Sales and hire:
Music Sales Distribution Centre,
Newmarket Road,
Bury St. Edmunds,
Suffolk IP33 3YB
England

Tel +44 (0)1284 702600
Fax +44 (0)1284 768301

www.musicsalesclassical.com

LUTOSŁAWSKI

Ministerstwo
Kultury
i Dziedzictwa
Narodowego.

instytut muzyki i tańca

This publication is based on source material from the Paul Sacher Foundation,
Witold Lutoslawski Collection, Basel.